■SCHOLASTIC
News
Nonfiction Readers

Snowy Weather Days

by Katie Marsico

Children's Press®
A Division of Scholastic Inc.
New York Toronto London Auckland Sydney
Mexico City New Delhi Hong Kong
Danbury, Connecticut

These content vocabulary word builders are for grades 1–2.
Subject Consultants: Robert Van Winkle, Chief Meteorologist, WBBH, Fort Myers, Florida; and Jack Williams, Public Outreach Coordinator, American Meteorological Society, Boston, Massachusetts

Reading Consultant: Cecilia Minden-Cupp, PhD, Former Director, Language and Literacy Program, Harvard Graduate School of Education, Cambridge, Massachusetts

Photographs © 2007: Alaska Stock Images/Calvin W. Hall: 21 bottom; AP/Wide World Photos: 5 bottom right, 6 (Miranda Meyer/Iowa City Gazette), 4 bottom left, 15 (Adam Nadel); Corbis Images: back cover, 20, 21 top (Theo Allofs/zefa), 5 bottom left, 7 (B.S.P.I.), 21 center (W. Perry Conway), 23 bottom right (Mike McQueen), 23 bottom left (Alexander Nemenov/epa), 5 top left, 8 (Royalty-Free), 1, 4 bottom right, 19 (Ariel Skelley), 23 top right (Joseph Sohm/Visions of America), 23 top left (Paul Souders); Index Stock Imagery: 4 top, 17 (AbleStock), 2, 9 (Mark Drewelow), 13 (Frank Siteman), 5 top right, 14 (Kathy Tarantola), 11 (Travel Ink Photo Library); Masterfile/Rick Gomez: cover.

Book Design: Simonsays Design!
Book Production: The Design Lab

Library of Congress Cataloging-in-Publication Data

Marsico, Katie, 1980–
Snowy weather days / Katie Marsico.
    p. cm. — (Scholastic news nonfiction readers)
Includes index.
ISBN-10: 0-531-16773-9
ISBN-13: 978-0-531-16773-1
1. Snow—Juvenile literature. I. Title. II. Series.
QC929.S7T78 2007
551.57'8—dc22   2006013306

1 2 3 4 5 6 7 8 9 10 R 16 15 14 13 12 11 10 09 08 07

CONTENTS

WORD HUNT

Look for these words as you read. They will be in **bold**.

blizzard
(**bliz**-urd)

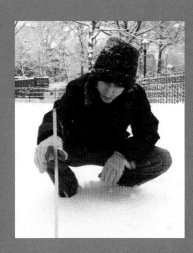

measure
(**meh**-shur)

sledding
(**sled**-ing)

clouds
(kloudz)

ruler
(**roo**-lur)

snow
(snoh)

snowflakes
(**snoh**-flayks)

It's Snowing!

When you step outside, huge, white **snowflakes** are falling everywhere!

Look around. The grass, trees, and sidewalk are all covered in **snow**!

snowflakes

Millions of snowflakes are covering this tree!

On cold, winter days, snow falls from **clouds** in the sky.

So, what is snow? When the air gets very cold, tiny drops of water freeze inside clouds. These drops stick together as they fall from the sky. They form snowflakes.

clouds

Snowflakes come in all shapes and sizes.

If it snows hard enough, it almost seems like a white blanket is covering the roofs and tree branches.

Have you ever been outside in this kind of weather?

It's fun to play outside after a heavy snowfall!

You can hear the crunch of new snow beneath your feet.

Sometimes, the snow may be so deep that you need a shovel to clear some of it away!

Grab your shovel! People need to clear the sidewalk if it snows hard enough.

Can you tell how much it has snowed?

People **measure** how deep snow is using a **ruler** or yardstick.

ruler

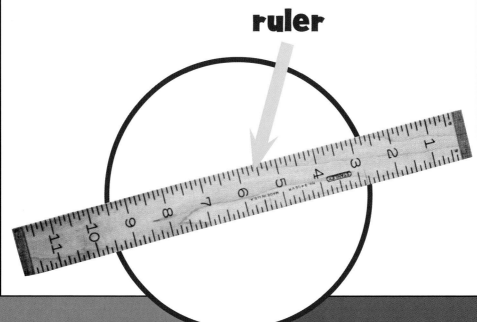

How deep is the snow? This boy is measuring to find out.

The wind can blow very hard when it snows.

Sometimes, wind pushes the snowflakes sideways. This causes a storm called a **blizzard**. A lot of snow falls during a blizzard.

Can you see past all that snow?
It's hard to see during a blizzard.

If there is a blizzard, your school may even close for the day! What will you do first?

Build a snowman?

Go **sledding**?

What is your favorite way to spend a snow day?

WHAT ELSE CAN YOU DO ON A SNOWY DAY?

You can study snowflakes! Did you know that snowflakes come in all shapes and sizes? Look out your window the next time it snows! Do you see any of the snowflakes shown here?

YOUR NEW WORDS

blizzard (**bliz**-urd) a heavy snowstorm

clouds (kloudz) white or gray masses that float in the sky and are made up of water and ice

measure (**meh**-shur) to figure out something's height, weight, or depth

ruler (**roo**-lur) a long, flat piece of wood or metal that is used for measuring things

sledding (**sled**-ing) a sport in which someone slides down a snowy hill on a sled

snow (snoh) weather that occurs when drops of water freeze inside clouds and fall to the ground

snowflakes (**snoh**-flayks) single flakes, or pieces, of snow

PLACES WHERE IT IS USUALLY VERY SNOWY

Alaska (United States)

Antarctica

Siberia

Switzerland

INDEX

FIND OUT MORE

Book:

Bauer, Marion Dane. *Snow*. New York, NY: Aladdin, 2003.

Website:

Kids Domain: Snow
http://www.kidsdomain.com/sports/snowsports/index.html

MEET THE AUTHOR:

Katie Marsico is a freelance writer and editor who lives with her family in Chicago, Illinois. Katie enjoys snowy weather, but she prefers being on a sunny beach in Florida with her mother, daughter, and husband.